FEATHERBOY AND THE BUFFALO

Written by Neil and Ting Morris
Illustrated by Anna Clarke
Historical advisor Marion Wood

Silver Burdett Company

First published 1984

Adapted and published in
the United States by
Silver Burdett Company,
Morristown, N.J.

1985 Printing

ISBN 0-382-06894-7
ISBN 0-382-06890-4 (lib. bindg.)

Library of Congress
Catalog Card No. 84-40840

Introduction

In prehistoric times hunters in search of food crossed the Bering Strait from Siberia, where northeast Asia meets northwest America. Much of the American continent was covered with ice, but as this began to melt people moved south over mountain ranges, through dense forests and fertile river valleys, and across wide plains and deserts. Wherever they went, these people adapted themselves to the area which they inhabited, developing skills and traditions best suited to the particular environment and its resources.

These were the Indians, so called later by Christopher Columbus when he thought that he had landed in the Indies. In the northeastern forests around the Great Lakes the Indians hunted deer, moose, bears and other animals, as well as fishing and growing maize. Along the northwest coast the Indians caught fish with hooks, nets and spears, and hunted seals and even whales with harpoons. In the rolling prairies and grasslands known as the Great Plains there were many nomadic tribes of Indians with different languages and customs. They were dependent for food, clothing and shelter on the buffalo, which they later hunted on horseback; horses had been brought to America by early Spanish settlers.

In the middle of the last century settlers flooded westwards across the plains, slaughtering whole herds of buffalo. In fear and anger the Indians fought the newcomers, but were defeated by the American army and restricted to reservations.

Every plains tribe was composed of several related bands of a hundred or more people, and in early summer the groups of each tribe came together in the open plains to hunt buffalo. This story is about a young Sioux Indian and his tribe's search for the buffalo. The information pages with the bow and arrow border will tell you more about the life of the plains people before the Indian wars.

Every spring groups of Sioux Indians traveled to their tribe's summer camp for the big buffalo hunt. Featherboy and Eagle-Eye were too young to hunt, but they looked forward to the exciting days ahead.

After their long ride the two boys were glad to see the smoke from the distant tepees. They thought of all the new friends they would make as they rode into camp.

But they were not given the usual warm welcome. There seemed to be a worried look on every face, and they wondered what could be wrong.

As Featherboy helped to put up their tepee, he heard another woman telling his mother about the problem. The hunters could not find any buffalo this year, and there was very little food left in the camp.

Next day the boys went off to join in a game with their friends. But Featherboy kept thinking about the gloom that hung over them like a black cloud.

Later he decided to explore beyond the camp. As it grew dark, he met the hunters returning. He could see from their faces that they had found no buffalo.

Early next morning Featherboy's father left with the hunters. Perhaps my father will bring them luck, he thought. Meanwhile he and Eagle-Eye went off with their friends to catch rabbits.

They stopped at a waterfall and splashed about in the icy water. Suddenly Featherboy saw three crows flying above him. It looked as if they were heading off into the hills.

Featherboy felt he had to follow the crows. They seemed to be leading him to the top of a hill, as if he would find something there.

Perhaps he would see buffalo in the valley below? Featherboy rushed on to the hilltop, but when he got there all he could see were rocks and bushes.

Featherboy was tired and disappointed. He lay down under a tree to rest and soon fell asleep.

He was awakened by the crows. When he saw them pecking at the juicy berries, he realized how hungry he was. He could pick some berries too – perhaps even take some back to camp.

Behind the bushes was a gaping hole, and at once Featherboy saw a great herd of buffalo. When he found a black feather, he remembered the crows and thought they must have shown him the way.

He picked up the feather and rushed back to the camp to tell everyone of his discovery. Featherboy was able to tell his father exactly where the buffalo were.

Featherboy's father took him at once to the chief's lodge. The chief and his hunters were preparing for a ceremony to help them find the buffalo. Now there would be a celebration instead!

That night the hunters danced in praise of the buffalo spirit. To thank him for his discovery, Featherboy was given a place of honor next to the chief.

Early next morning the hunters moved in for the kill. Although Featherboy, Eagle-Eye and the other boys were too young to hunt, they were very excited as they waited for their chance to help skin the buffalo.

The hunt was a great success, and now there was plenty of food for the whole tribe. As Featherboy sat and ate, he secretly thanked the crows for leading him and his people to the buffalo.

Tepees and travois

The Sioux tribe lived on the American plains. Each family's home was a tent called a tepee. This was made by putting buffalo skins around wooden poles, leaving a smoke hole at the top. The tepees were always put up so that the door faced east.

Plains Indians were traveling people. Women made and packed the travois, which were vehicles made from tepee poles. These were pulled by horses, and smaller ones by dogs. Young children were carried in wooden cages on the travois.

Picture writing

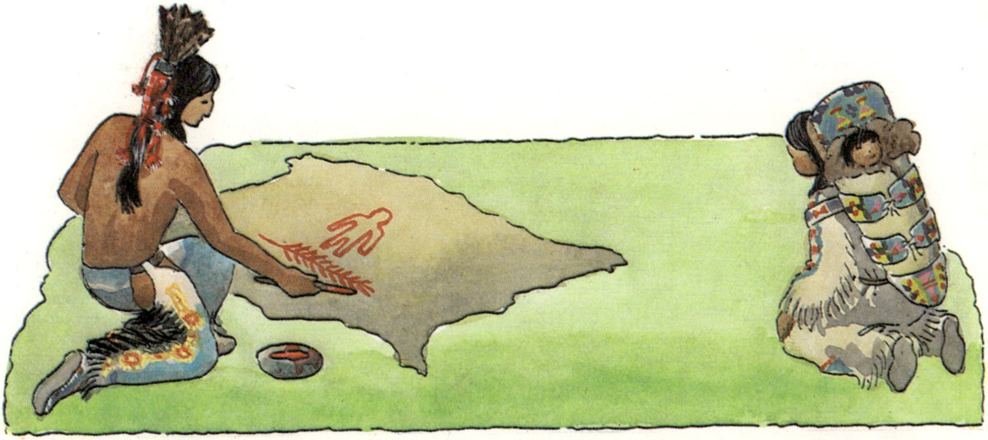

A child was often named after a special event, an object, or something that happened in a dream. The child's name could then be written in a picture. Featherboy's name could have looked like this.

peace

war

strong

speak

listen

see

frog

fingers

camp

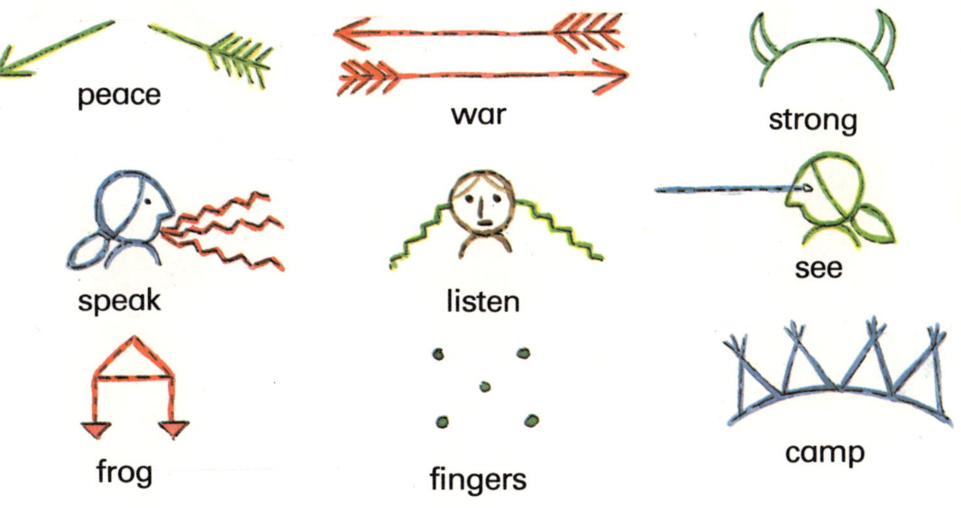

The Indians used pictures instead of writing to record the important events in their lives. Stories about the tribe were often drawn in pictures on buffalo skin.

The buffalo

The Plains Indians needed the buffalo for their way of life. They used every part of the animal, and nothing was wasted. All these things were made from the buffalo:
1 skin blanket; 2 horns; 3 shirt, leggings and moccasins; 4 horn mace; 5 knife sheath; 6 shield; 7 tongue hairbrush; 8 bone scraper; 9 sinew cord; 10 tail fly-whisk; 11 tepee skin; 12 hide box; 13 parfleche (hide container); 14 dung fuel; 15 stomach for cooking; 16 horn spoon; 17 bag; 18 dress; 19 cradle.

Dances

There were dances for many occasions. The Sun Dance was held when the tribe met in the summer. In one dance the dancer had his chest pierced by wooden skewers attached to a decorated pole. He leaned back gazing at the sun and danced to the beat of a drum until the skewers tore from his skin. This pain was suffered so that the great spirit would send the tribe health and food.

Sioux hunters did the Bear Dance to ask the bear spirit for help before they went on a hunt.

Hunting buffalo

Indians hunted the buffalo on foot as well as on horseback. Sometimes the hunters wore wolf skins to get as close as possible and then use their lance or bow. The bull buffalo did not fear wolves and faced them if they came near.

Sometimes the Indians stampeded a group of buffalo towards a ravine. Before they could stop, the animals thundered over the edge.

This map of North America shows where the tribes in these stories lived.

Phototypeset by Kalligraphics Limited,
Redhill, Surrey, England

1 2 3 4 5 6 7 8 9 10– L B –93 92 91 90 89 88 87 86 85